MW00976681

"When an expecting mother receives the frightening news that the gift of God in her womb has a poor or fatal prognosis, it evokes many questions and emotions. Here is a Scripture study designed to help process and bring guidance during this season of pain and decision-making. Kim Endraske uses the pain of her own story woven with the timeless truths of God's Word to bring hope, healing and direction to mothers in a similar position she was in with the loss of her precious son Tommy. You will find a great friend in Kim who will point you to a Greater Friend as you work your way through this excellent resource of hope during this season of uncertainty."

Nick Brown -- Lead Pastor, Collierville Bible Church
Certified Biblical Counselor with ACBC

A Child of Promise:

A Bible Study for Parents
Facing a Poor or Fatal Prognosis
for their Unborn Child

by Kim Endraske

+ *Kim Endraske*
2 Cor. 1:2-10

A Child of Promise

Copyright © 2014 Kim Endraske

All rights reserved.

ISBN: 150049285X
ISBN-13: 978-1500492854

Scripture quotations are from The Holy Bible, English Standard Version (ESV®),
copyright © 2001 by Crossway, a publishing ministry of Good News Publishers.
Used by permission. All rights reserved.

Dedication

This book is dedicated to my Savior and Lord,
my Great Shepherd,
Jesus Christ.

He sought me when I was lost.
He pulled me out of the pit.
He set my feet upon the rock.
He died for me while I was still a sinner.
He has made beauty out of these ashes.

"I thank him who has given me strength, Christ Jesus our Lord,
because he judged me faithful,
appointing me to his service,
though formerly I was a blasphemer,
persecutor, and insolent opponent ...
To the King of the ages, immortal, invisible, the only God,
be honor and glory forever and ever. Amen."
1 Timothy 1:12,17

In Loving Memory of
Thomas William Endraske

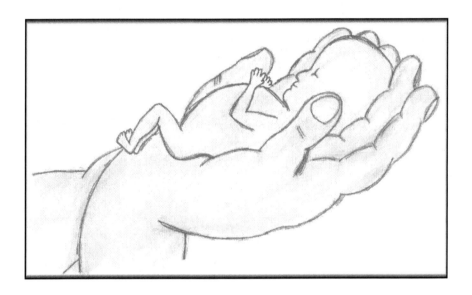

September 15, 1998
Budded on Earth to Bloom in Heaven

Artwork by Kim Endraske

A Child of Promise

My oldest daughter, Emily, grew up singing this little children's song, "I am a Promise" by the Gaither Vocal Band. At the time I thought to myself, "How can a little girl or a little boy <u>be</u> a promise?"

In everyday speech, the word *promise* has two basic meanings.

One, that a person will carry out what they have told you, such as, "I promise to take you out for ice cream tonight." The second meaning is that of a cause for hope in the future, such as, "That artist shows great promise."

When my unborn son, Tommy, was diagnosed with a condition deemed incompatible with life, it caused me to question all kinds of things. So many of those questions hinged on these two meanings for promise.

* Would God keep His promises?
* Did Tommy's future hold promise?

The answer to both of these questions is a resounding, "Yes!" God would indeed keep His promises. He would without question walk this lonely road with me. And, Tommy's life, no matter how short or long it might be, still held promise. His life had meaning and purpose even if he would never take a breath of air in this world.

This ministry was named "A Child of Promise" because I wanted to encourage families to stand firm that even if it feels like the world is crashing down around you, you can trust in God's promises for you and for your child.

Thank you

Where do I begin to thank all of the people who helped make this possible?

I cannot thank my husband and children enough for their patience and endurance during the countless hours that I have spent working on this.

I thank my sister for always remembering Tommy's birthday and for her many prayers and encouraging words over the last sixteen years (and more)!

Thanks also go out to the many individuals, families and organizations who have ministered to me in my grief, as well as in writing this book.

Contents

Dear Friend,

This study has been a work in the making for well over ten years.

When I learned that my son Tommy had posterior urethral valves, a fatal condition preventing him from passing urine, I had only known I was pregnant for six weeks! I found myself suddenly thrown in a whole slew of circumstances I was completely unprepared for. In fact, nothing could have possibly prepared me for the days and weeks ahead.

Each lesson is broken into reflecting on a stage of your pregnancy, as well as your baby's birth and the years ahead. Take your time, savoring every moment in God's Word.

My story is unique, as is yours. God has created each one of us, and each one of our children, uniquely with a special purpose and plan.

I pray that this study will bring you peace and wisdom as you draw close to the One who made all creation. May God's word be a healing balm to your heart and may you be comforted in knowing that you are not alone in this journey.

Fondly,

Kim

Pregnancy

After three months of trying to get pregnant, and four negative pregnancy tests, I finally saw those two little lines every woman wishing to be pregnant hungers for. I was pregnant!

In my human plan, I wanted two perfect kids spaced a perfect three years apart. Here it was! The answer to my prayer! The baby we'd been trying to conceive was due just one month before our daughter's third birthday.

We immediately started planning for this little one.

How would we tell people? Would it be a boy or a girl? What would we name him, or her? Where would he (or she) sleep? How would we decorate the nursery?

I could hardly wait to share the good news, but March (when our baby was due) sounded like a long way off.

To complicate matters, we were temporarily without insurance as my husband had just started a new job after being out of work for over two months. I had suffered a miscarriage three years earlier and found myself wishing for the reassurance of a healthy ultrasound.

We shared the good news with our family and friends immediately. Our two-year-old daughter, Emily, loved telling everyone, "I gonna be a big sister!" Two weeks later we went in for a preliminary ultrasound. I was already eight weeks along and we saw a tiny heartbeat in a tiny gummy bear.

Each chapter will begin with an excerpt from my own pregnancy journey. Then, it will be turned over to you.

"Your turn" will begin with general reflection on this stage of pregnancy from your perspective and then you will be directed to relevant passages of scripture.

Let me urge you to spend time in prayer before, during and after your time in the Word. Ask the Holy Spirit to reveal truth to you and to penetrate your heart, soul and mind as you search the scriptures.

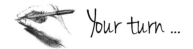 Your turn ...

What preparations have gone into this pregnancy?

How did you feel when you first learned you were pregnant?

How did you tell your family? How did they react?

What future dreams did you already have for this baby?

Read 1 Samuel 1 and respond to the following questions.

Who closed Hannah's womb? (v. 5)

How was Elkanah's other wife, Peninnah, treating Hannah? (v. 6)

How was Hannah feeling and behaving? (v. 7-8)

Did you struggle to conceive this pregnancy?

How did that make you feel?

How was Hannah feeling and behaving as she prayed at the temple (v. 10-16)?

How did she feel and behave after her prayer and talk with Eli? (v. 18-19)

Why did Hannah name her son Samuel? (v. 20)

Read and reflect on Psalm 139.

Take some time to copy here or into your own journal a few verses that really minister to you.

What speaks to you in this psalm?

Suspicion

My obstetrician scheduled me for another visit a month later when I would be twelve weeks along. Incredibly, my doctor did ultrasounds every month and I couldn't wait to see how my baby had grown.

The day before I went in, I shared with a dear friend over the phone that I was worried something was wrong with the baby. I feared that I would learn something at this ultrasound that I didn't want to know. The sense of foreboding I had was intense. In my heart, I just 'knew' something was wrong.

Of course, my friend (and my husband) assured me that I was worrying over nothing, that the baby would be fine and I should put my mind at rest.

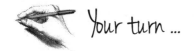 Your turn ...

Did you have any sense that something might be wrong?

How did that feeling express itself?

Did you share this with anyone? What was their reaction?

Read Isaiah 40 and respond to the following questions:

Describe in your own words the "bigness" of God.

How does Isaiah describe the power of God compared with the weakness of mankind?

What is the Lord's blessing on those who wait for Him (v. 31)?

Read Psalm 86 and respond to the following questions:

Are you feeling poor and needy? In need of joy?

Who is the only one who can fill those needs?

Who did David call upon to in his need?

Where have you been turning?

Do you find yourself struggling to praise God's name? Take time now to give God your praise. List here reasons why He is worthy of your praise.

Meditate on verse 17. Ask God for a sign of His goodness.

Who are your enemies that you would like to see this sign? Pray for them now.

Read and reflect on Philippians 4:4-13.

Take some time to copy here or into your own journal a few verses that really speak to you.

What are you feeling anxious about? Let your requests be made known to God.

Tests

The next day I went in for my twelve-week check. My husband and daughter were with me. They, too, couldn't wait to see our precious little one. I remember my bladder being so full and I remember the nurse having a terrible time drawing blood. The container wouldn't fit on right and my blood spilled out, running down my arm. I worried that my husband or daughter would faint and I felt so sorry for them, as yet unaware of what sorrow lay just ahead for us.

The instant the doctor turned on the ultrasound, the screen filled with my little baby, a little baby with an enormous balloon inside his belly. His abdomen was one big, black circle. I gasped, raising a finger timidly toward the screen, "What is that in his belly?"

After several more minutes of searching the screen, the doctor said, *"We're going to need more tests. I want you to go in for another ultrasound. I'm not sure exactly what is wrong, but it's something in the baby's abdomen, probably his bladder or maybe his intestines. I'm going to refer you to a specialist for more tests. Try to take it easy this weekend and we'll find out more Monday."*

Monday brought more tests. I lay on the table for an hour of ultrasounds by several different people. That afternoon I returned for an amniocentesis, a procedure I'd been certain I would never have! The idea of that long needle piercing into my belly had me scared out of my mind. I feared it might hurt our unborn baby, rupture my amniotic sac or bring on labor. And yet, I was determined to do whatever needed to be done for my little one.

 Your turn ...

What tests did you have done?

What did they show?

How did you feel during the tests and while waiting for the results?

Read about God's promises to Abram in Genesis 12:1-9, 15:1-6, 16:1-4, 17:1-8, 17:15-27, 18:1-15, 21:1-7

Have you ever laughed at the miracles of God? How?

In what ways do you now feel the need to "help" God?

Read Romans 4:16-25 and think about how this compares with what you've just read.

What did Abraham consider, but still not weaken in faith? (v. 19)

What was he fully convinced of? (v. 21)

What was his faith counted to him as? (v. 22)

As time allows, in the coming weeks, read the entire book of Romans, particularly chapters 1-8. Read it over and over again. Meditate on the truths held in these pages.

Read Genesis 22:1-18 and answer the following questions.

How might Abraham have felt as he heard God tell him to sacrifice Isaac?

Describe how you relate to this passage during this time.

Imagine Abraham's face as he looks into his son's eyes as he is bound on the altar. Try drawing it.

Now read Hebrews 11:1-19 and respond to the following questions:

What is the definition of faith? (v. 1)

How did the people of old receive their commendation? (v. 2)

What is it impossible to do without faith? (v. 6)

How did Sarah consider God who had promised? (v. 11)

What did Abraham consider God able to do? (v. 19)

Psalm 44:21 says, "For he [God] knows the secrets of the heart." Since God already knew Abraham's heart, why might God have tested Abraham in this way?

I once heard that so much of God's testing of us is not to prove our faith to HIM, but to prove it to *us*. Pray about the truth of this. What are your thoughts?

Let's keep looking together as this word, testing.

Read 1 Peter 1:3-9 and respond to the following questions:

Look carefully at verse 6. What are you to rejoice in? (see verse 5)

What is more precious than gold? (v. 7)

What will the tested genuineness of your faith result in? (v. 7)

What is another outcome of your faith? (v. 9)

This would be a great passage to memorize or write down somewhere to keep with you and encourage you. Try reciting this passage out loud every morning and night. See how the Lord speaks to you through it.

Ultimately, friends, your faith cannot be proved genuine, if it is not genuine.

1 Peter 1:3 tells us that God has caused us to be born again to a living hope through the resurrection of Jesus Christ. Do you believe that?

Have you confessed and repented of your sin and found forgiveness by the shed blood of Jesus?

Have you trusted in Jesus Christ as your Savior and Lord?

Remember that the outcome of your faith is the salvation of your souls (1 Peter 1:9) and without faith it is impossible to please God (Hebrews 11:6).

> *"For God so loved the world, that he gave his only Son, that whoever believes in him should not perish but have eternal life. For God did not send his Son into the world to condemn the world, but in order that the world might be saved through him. Whoever believes in him is not condemned, but whoever does not believe is condemned already, because he has not believed in the name of the only Son of God."* John 3:16-18

Please let me appeal to you that the most important decision you can ever make is to put your faith fully in the Lord Jesus Christ. If you have any questions about this, I would love to talk with you.

I remember what it felt like to be without hope, without faith. If that is you right now, I pray that today is the day you will seek the Lord with your whole heart, that your faith will be made genuine.

Read James 1:1-12 and respond to the following questions:

Why are we able to count it all joy when we meet trials of various kinds? (v. 3)

What is the full effect of that steadfastness that the testing of our faith produces? (v. 4)

What is the blessing for those remaining steadfast under trial, which God has promised to those who love Him? (v. 12)

Please, I want you to stop right now and pray for God to help you to remain steadfast during this time to testing and trial.

Father, there are so many things to think about, so many questions and decisions to make. Please, help me to walk by faith. Grant me wisdom. Help me to trust in You and not give way to fear and doubt. Give me the strength to persevere and remain steadfast.

The book of Romans closes with this, "*Now to him who is able to strengthen you according to my gospel and the preaching of Jesus Christ, according to the revelation of the mystery that was kept secret for long ages but has now been disclosed and through the prophetic writings has been made known to all nations, according to the command of the eternal God, to bring about the obedience of faith-- to the only wise God be glory forevermore through Jesus Christ! Amen.*" (Romans 16:25-27)

So often our struggles with obedience are tied to a simple lack of trust. Oftentimes I see my children struggling to believe that I have their best interest at heart.

Dear friend, trust God. He is able. He is faithful. He is good. He is worthy of your trust. He has your best interests at heart.

Think about this idea of the obedience of faith. Reflect on a time you've seen someone, even a child, struggling to obey. How can you see yourself now in their struggles?

Read and reflect on Psalm 27.

Pray this psalm out loud to the Lord. Take some time to copy here or into your own journal a few verses that really minister to you.

Pour out your heart to God here. Pour out your pain, and your praise.

Prognosis

"Mrs. Endraske, the fetus is a boy, but I don't think he will survive. He has a condition that is incompatible with life. There is a blockage in his urethra which is preventing his bladder from emptying. Amniotic fluid is made up of this fluid and without it, your baby's lungs cannot develop.

Also, it appears that his kidneys are already failing. Most likely your body will keep him alive until he is born. His lungs will not have developed and he will be unable to breathe."

These unbelievable words were spoken to me in a little, white counseling room. The room seemed filled up by its single square box of tissues on a simple metal desk and standard order telephone. My mother-in-law sat quietly next to me, as my husband was out of town in training for his new job.

How could this be happening to me?

I was lost.

What happened to my two perfect children, three perfect years apart?

 Your turn ...

What have you been told about your baby's condition?

How did you react?

Where were you when you heard the news?

Was anyone with you when you were told? How did that help or hinder?

Is there anything that could have been done differently to make it easier on you to hear?

Read Luke 1-2, imagining yourself in Elizabeth's and Mary's shoes. Then answer the following questions:

What does the angel say to Zechariah? (Luke 1:13-17)

How does Zechariah initially respond? (Luke 1:18)

What is Elizabeth's reaction? (Luke 1:25)

What does the angel say to Mary? (Luke 1:30-33)

What is Mary's reaction? (Luke 1:34)

Copy down Mary's response to the angel in Luke 1:38

What is God asking you to do right now?

Can you, like Mary, say, "I am the servant of the Lord; let it be to me according to your word?"

Look carefully at the interaction between Mary and Elizabeth in Luke 1:39-45. What jumps out at you in this passage?

Copy Luke 1:45 here.

What does Simeon say to Mary when the infant Jesus is brought into the temple? (Luke 2:34-35)

Look again at Luke 2:19 and Luke 2:51. What is Mary doing with this knowledge?

Sometimes people tell us that our future will be bright and glorious and amazing. Sometimes people tell us that our future will be gloomy and rough and painful.

Reflect on a time when someone predicted future glory for you. Write about how this affected you.

Now, reflect on this time as future pain is being predicted for you. How is this affecting you now?

Read Isaiah 45:9-12 and answer the following questions:

Who made your child?

How does that impact the way you view your child's prognosis?

How does this passage make you feel?

How have you been quarreling with God?

Read Hebrews 12:1-4 and respond to the following questions:

What was Jesus looking toward while He endured the cross? (v. 2)

What are we to consider? (v.3) Why?

What do you learn from these verses?

Re-read Genesis 22:12.

What do you find yourself withholding from God? Pray for God to give you the strength to give it all to Him.

Read John 18-20, considering the betrayal, crucifixion, death, burial and resurrection of Jesus.

Take some time to thank God for His sacrifice, to thank Jesus for His obedience and suffering. Pray for the Lord to give you the strength to endure, that you would not grow weary or fainthearted.

Journal about anything from these chapters that speak to you right now.

Read and reflect on Psalm 42.

Take some time to copy here or into your own journal a few verses that really minister to you.

Are you feeling downcast? Where is your hope?

Questions

"Mrs. Endraske, you have three options. You can terminate the pregnancy, you can do nothing and let nature take its course, or we can attempt an in-utero procedure to try to bypass the bladder obstruction."

In the midst of my confusion over the first two "options," my ears perked up. My mind started spinning. Did he say in-utero procedure? You mean, they can fix this?

"Hooray," I thought, "my perfect family is back in the picture!"

"Doctor, termination is not an option for us. We will not end this baby's life. But, please, I don't want to go through the next six months waiting for the day my baby will die. Please, do something to help him. What can you do for him? Can you save him?"

The doctor produced a blank piece of plain, white typing paper and began with a pen to outline our surgical options. They could use a laser beam to open a tiny hole in the end of the baby's urethra, burning out the obstruction; or they could insert a shunt to drain his bladder out the side of his belly into the amniotic sac, bypassing the obstruction; or they could wait until he was bigger and remove him from my womb for surgical correction and then replace him for the remainder of the pregnancy.

All of these options had their risks: rupturing the sac, infection and premature labor – but at least we had some real options, options that most of you reading this do not have.

My mind was consumed with all the unanswered questions about my son's condition.

* What caused it?

* Had I done something wrong?

* Do babies with this ever live?

* Is it genetic?

* How common is it?

I was also full of questions about our surgical options, like:

* What are the statistical rates of success?

* Are there risks for me?

* Does it hurt the baby?

* Is it painful?

* How many times have these doctors done this before?

* What if it didn't work?

 Your turn ...

What questions are filling your mind?

Where have you gone for answers to your questions?

How have you felt about those answers?

Read Isaiah 55:8-9 and answer the following questions:

In what ways are God's thoughts not like ours?

What are you thinking about today? Write out some of your thoughts right now.

Read Proverbs 3:5-6 and answer the following questions:

How are we called to trust in God?

What are we not to lean on?

What are we to do in all our ways?

Read Proverbs 14:12 and copy it here.

How does this verse relate to the Proverbs 3:5-6 passage?

As humans, it is natural for us to lean on our own understanding. We want to do what seems right to us, but God wants us to trust in Him. His wisdom is always better than ours.

How are you struggling to trust in God right now?

At this moment, is there a way that seems right to you, or to others, but its end is the way to death? Describe.

Write about a time when God has shown Himself worthy of being trusted in your past.

Read 1 Corinthians 1:18-2:16 and respond to the following questions:

What is the word of the cross to those who are perishing? (v. 1:18)

What about to those who are being saved? (v. 1:18)

What does Paul not want their faith to rest in? What does Paul want their faith to rest in? (v. 2:5)

How are you struggling today to put your faith in the power and wisdom of God rather than of man?

Read and reflect on Psalm 77.

Take some time to copy here or in your own journal a few verses that really minister to you.

How do you see the author wrestling with pain and praise?

Decisions

I knew that I could not end my baby's life, but I also dreaded submitting myself to a surgical procedure for a baby who might not survive either way. I had never been under anesthesia before. As a matter of fact, I'd never even had stitches before.

What was I supposed to do? What was the best choice to make when none of my choices were good?

This was the one place, though, where I did have a choice.

I didn't have a choice in Tommy being created with posterior urethral valves, but I did have a choice now about what to do.

I knew that these choices would affect the rest of not only my life and his life, but my husband's life, his big sister's life, even our extended family's lives.

For so many parents, this is the one of the most difficult times in their pregnancy. They are being placed in a position to make life-altering decisions for their unborn child and they simply don't know what to do.

They hardly know this little one. They don't want to get attached, only to have their baby taken from them. They certainly don't want their child going through pain, but they don't want to go through pain either.

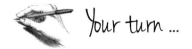 Your turn ...

What options are you being given about your baby's future?

What was your first impulse in the choices you have to make?

How have those initial reactions remained or are you wavering in your decisions?

Who have you talked with about the decisions you are faced with?

How have they helped or hurt in making these decisions?

I'd like you to stop right now and pray for the Lord to give you His perfect, divine, holy wisdom, that you would be able to make the choices that would be pleasing in His sight, that would be best for your baby, for your family and for the name of Jesus. Pray to make choices that you will be able to have confidence in, without wavering or regretting them in the future.

Read Deuteronomy 30:11-20 and answer the following questions:

How does this passage make you feel?

How can things be so black and white?

Look deeply in verse 16. What is the key to walking in God's ways and keeping His commandments?

Read Matthew 27:1-5 and answer the following questions:

How did Judas feel after betraying Jesus? What did he say to the elders and priests? (v. 3-4)

How does this apply to the decisions you are having to make now?

What did Judas do after speaking to the priests and elders? (v. 5)

How do you imagine a parent might feel after making decisions that lead to shortening the life of their unborn child?

Read 1 Peter 3:13-17 and answer the following questions:

Who are we not to fear? (v. 13-14)

Who are we to honor? (v. 15)

What are we to be prepared to do? (v. 15)

In what ways are you suffering now?

Copy verse 17 here:

How does this relate to the choices before you right now?

Many people around you might believe that ending your pregnancy will put an end to your suffering. Maybe you are wrestling with those feelings right now. What are your thoughts?

Has anyone questioned your decision to continue your pregnancy? Were you able to answer them with gentleness and respect and with a good conscience? Describe.

Pray for God to give you opportunities to share the hope that is in you with others. You can expect that some people will not understand your decision to continue your pregnancy. Ask God to give you joy in the face of this added pain. Pray also to have compassion and love for other families you meet who are being faced with these same decisions.

Read 1 John 3:16-24 and answer the following questions:

How do we know love? (v. 16)

How are we not to love? How are we to love? (v. 18)

How can you lay down your life for your brother right now?

Who is greater than our hearts? Who knows everything? (v. 20)

Who can we have confidence before? (v. 20)

Read and reflect on Psalm 19.

Take some time to copy here or into your own journal a few verses that really minister to you.

How does this psalm speak to your spirit right now?

Waiting

After being told that Tommy would surely die without extraordinary measures -- or a miracle -- I began thinking of the long months that lay before me until Tommy would be born. Waiting for the amniocentesis results, waiting for the in-utero procedure to be done, waiting for my son's birth, waiting for my son to be healed ... or to die. There were so many different things I was waiting for, but none of them were anticipated with the excitement I'd experienced while waiting to get pregnant.

On Thursday, September 10, 1998, I underwent an in-utero procedure in an attempt to either insert a stent to drain Tommy's bladder into the amniotic sac, or to laser an opening in the urethra.

Unfortunately, the surgery was unsuccessful. Tommy was still so small and his position in my uterus made it impossible to perform the procedure.

After turning off the ultrasound machine guiding their instruments, my doctor asked me to return on Monday so he could check to see if Tommy's heart was still beating. He wasn't sure he would make it.

That was the longest weekend of my life. Those four days of waiting were sheer agony. They were truly a low point on this roller coaster ride. I cried buckets. I felt sick to the core. Was my sweet baby boy going to die?

In the car on the way to the hospital, I had prayed for God to either heal Tommy, or take him quickly. Now it looked like he was about to die and I wasn't ready. I wanted him so badly.

All weekend I struggled with deciding whether I would attempt the procedure again or not when Tommy got bigger.

For many of you, the waiting will be long. Weeks. Months. But for others, the waiting will be over quickly and unexpectedly.

I spent much of that weekend researching Tommy's medical condition and beginning to plan a memorial service for him. I had little hope that the news on Monday would be good.

How will you spend your time waiting? You never know the day the waiting will end, and the rollercoaster ride of pregnancy will be over. Ask God to prepare your heart.

If you are currently in this stage of waiting, let me urge you spend this time in preparation and prayer. Treasure these times with your little one in your heart. Use this time to draw close to Jesus. Use it to plan a beautiful birth. Keep a journal so you can remember these days. Sit in patient, expectant silence at the Lord's feet.

Friend, I understand that your baby's birth will bring with it a bittersweet joy. Whether born alive or born still, whether fully healed or not, you will meet this long awaited baby face to face for the first time and that arrival will bring with it joy, though tinged with sorrow.

 Your turn ...

How long have you been waiting?

Has there been anything constructive you have been able to do during your waiting time?

What kinds of reactions have you received from friends and family during this time of waiting?

How have you handled curious questions from those close, or not so close, to you?

Daily I am engaged in a battle, and so are you. There is a battle being waged all around us, but there is also a battle being waged inside our own minds. This is where many battles will be won and lost.

Read 2 Corinthians 10:3-5 and answer the following questions:

How are we not to wage war?

How are we to wage war?

Read Ephesians 6:10-18 and answer the following questions:

How will you be able to stand against the devil? (v. 10-13)

How do you extinguish the evil one's flaming darts? (v. 16)

What is your helmet? (v. 17)

What is your sword? (v. 17)

How are you going to fight this battle today, tomorrow and in the many days to come? Make a battle plan.

Read Romans 12:1-2 and answer the following questions:

What is our spiritual worship? (v. 1)

How are we transformed? (v. 2)

Read 1 Peter 1:13-16 and answer the following questions:

What are we to prepare our minds for? (v. 13)

How can we prepare our minds?

What are we to set our hope on? (v. 13)

What are we not to be conformed to? (v. 14 – and Romans 12:2)

We are called to be holy. Why? (v. 15-16)

Read 1 John 4:4 and relate this to 1 Peter 1.

Read Matthew 6:25-34 and answer the following questions:

Do you find yourself worrying about tomorrow? What specific thoughts are filling your mind?

Why do we not need to worry about the future?

What are we to seek first? (v. 33)

What do you find yourself seeking?

Read 2 Samuel 12:13-23 and answer the following questions:

In this instance, why did David's child become sick? *(For more background read 2 Samuel 11-12.)*

How do you feel when you read this?

When David's child became sick, what did David do? (v. 16)

How did David react after being told his child is dead? (v. 20)

Why did David's behavior change? (vs. 22-23)

Look at verse 23. Will David see his son again? Where?

Read John 9:1-7 and answer the following questions:

What is the assumption behind the disciples' question in verse 2?

What is Jesus' response to them in verse 3?

How does this relate to what you have just read in 2 Samuel?

Read through Matthew 8-9.

In these chapters, Jesus performs many miracles. God has not changed. God can still perform miracles. Is God calling you to pray for a miracle in your baby's life? Use the space below to pour your heart out in faith to God.

Read and reflect on Psalm 22.

Take some time to copy here or into your own journal a few verses that really minister to you.

How do you see the author wrestling with pain and praise?

Birth

Monday morning I returned to the hospital. The ultrasound technician sat silently searching the black screen.

Tommy looked different. His bladder was smaller and I couldn't see the telltale fluttering heartbeat. I asked the technician if she saw the heartbeat. Her answer was to get the doctor, who informed me that Tommy had already passed away.

My fears had come true. My son. My precious baby boy had died.

Within an hour I'd left the hospital, carrying a prescription for a medication to start contractions and a container to hold Tommy's remains should he be delivered before I made it back.

My first stop in my shocked state was to retrieve my daughter from preschool. Picking Emily up, I headed to a fast food play place. I needed some time to think and I needed to see her sunshiny face.

My mind was filled with morbid thoughts. The idea that I was carrying a dead baby inside of me was horrific. I felt like a living tomb for my unborn baby. I imagined what the smiling mommies around me would think if they knew that the baby I was carrying was dead.

Shortly after taking my first dose of induction medication, I started bleeding. That very night I returned to the hospital to begin the process of giving birth to a baby who would never cry, never take a breath, never gaze into my grieving face.

At 3:35 a.m., on September 15, 1998, Thomas William Endraske was born into the world.

I thank God for blessing me with a wonderful nurse. Pat had been my nurse during the in-utero procedure and she recognized me immediately when I returned. She shared with me that she had suffered seven pregnancy losses and she encouraged me to see Tommy when he was born. I am so incredibly thankful for this valuable piece of advice because in so many ways we were totally unprepared. Everything had happened so quickly. The past 24 hours had been a blur.

We hadn't even thought to bring a camera to the hospital. It was the middle of the night. Tommy was delivered by a resident that I'd never met before. I was at a total loss for how to handle his birth.

The dark, silent room was filled with nothing but emptiness. Where was the joy and noise and excited chaos like when my daughter Emily was born?

Remembering Pat's encouragement, I insisted on seeing Tommy. I was shown him for only a moment but that image has remained with me for all these years. His lifeless body was held out for my inspection, lying flat splayed out on a blanket. It felt like I was evaluating a piece of meat at the butcher's shop.

Despite my pain, my son, even at that moment, had already left this world and was in the presence of Jesus. He was home and I was left to return the next day to my own home with aching arms and an aching heart.

 Your turn ...

Describe your child's birth.

Did you receive any advice or encouragement that was helpful?

Did you have any regrets? Were you able to remedy them?

What were the happiest moments?

Read Job 1-2 and answer the following questions:

How does God describe Job? (Job 1:8)

What does Satan think will happen to Job if God removes His protection? (Job 1:11)

What is God's response to Satan's challenge? (Job 1:12)

What do the four messengers report to Job? (Job 1:14-19)

What is Job's response? (Job 1:20-22)

Reread Job 1:8 and Job 2:3. What did God say to Satan?

How does this make you feel?

What is Job's wife's response to all this calamity? (Job 2:9)

Has anyone around you responded like that? Describe.

How did Job's three friends initially respond to Job? (Job 2:11-13)

Has anyone around you responded like that? Describe.

As time permits, read the rest of the book of Job. Consider how Job responds to his grief, how his friends respond, how God answers them. Study how in chapter 42, the Lord restores Job's fortune, giving him twice as much as he had before. You might particularly notice that God gives Job double the number of sheep, camels, oxen and donkeys, but He only gives Job seven more sons and seven more daughters. Pray through this. Why would that number still be twice what Job had before?

After reading 2 Samuel about David's son's death, John 9 about the man born blind, and now reading Job 1-2, summarize what you have learned in these three passages.

Read John 16:16-24 and answer the following questions:

Look at verse 20. Why will the disciples be weeping? What will happen to their sorrow?

How do you agree or disagree with the idea that after the baby is delivered, the mother no longer remembers the pain of childbirth for the joy that the baby has been born?

Read and reflect on Psalm 71.

Take some time to copy here or into your own journal a few verses that really minister to you.

What will your mouth tell of?

Ultimately, whether in your child's miraculous healing or untimely death or something in between, God has created your child with a purpose. I pray that your child's birth will mark the beginning of a remarkable journey, with the Holy Spirit leading the way.

After

Though my son's life had ended, the choices I needed to make had not. For example, I still had to decide whether to have an autopsy or not. I had to figure out what arrangements I would like for his body and whether or not to send out birth announcements.

The days that followed Tommy's birth day were filled with planning a memorial service and spreading the news to family and friends that our baby boy had died. We looked forward to a service that would pay honor to our son's brief life, giving us a time to share our love for him with others that we loved. This season of our life was coming to a close.

My father-in-law constructed a beautiful little wooden casket and my mom sewed a baby blanket for Tommy's tiny body to be wrapped in. Our Sunday School teacher spoke on the hope of heaven, based on the book, <u>Mommy, Please Don't Cry</u> by Linda deYvaz, which I had read at my 16-month-old nephew's funeral a year earlier. Several special songs were sung including the hymn, "Because He Lives." At the conclusion of the service, our daughter, Emily, released two blue balloons. We watched them rise and disappear in the clear blue sky.

For many of you, there will be days, weeks, months or years of changed dreams ahead of you. You may find yourself now facing ongoing health issues – deciding whether or not to provide life support, what special treatments your child needs, and learning all you can about how to take care of your new son or daughter.

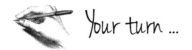 Your turn ...

What decisions have you had to make since your child's birth?

How did you go about making them?

What painful situations or regrets do you find yourself coping with?

What have been the most peaceful or joyful moments since your child's birth?

Read and reflect on John 11:1-44. Read the whole passage through first, then come back to answer the questions.

John 11:5-6 reads, *"Now Jesus loved Martha and her sister and Lazarus. So, when he heard Lazarus was ill, he stayed two days longer in the place where he was."*

If Jesus loved them, why would he wait two more days?

How are you struggling with believing that Jesus loves you, too?

Read verse 15 again. Why is Jesus glad He wasn't there? What does Jesus want his disciples to believe?

Cry out to God. He is near you even when you cannot see Him.

What does God want you to believe?

Read verse 19 again. What had many of the Jews come to do?

What consolation have you received? From whom? How have your family and friends ministered to you?

Write out verses 25-27.

Reread verses 33-35.

How was Jesus feeling? Why? How do you think Jesus feels as He sees you cry?

Answer the question asked in verse 37.

Read and reflect on Isaiah 49:13-16.

Why are the heavens and earth to sing for joy?

Who will God have compassion on?

How did the people of Zion feel? (v. 14)

Does it feel like God has forgotten you?

This passage compares God forgetting His people to a woman forgetting her nursing child. Can you imagine forgetting your baby?

Where has God engraved your name?
The name of your baby?

Write your names on the hand to the right.

"Beloved, do not be surprised at the fiery trial when it comes upon you to test you, as though something strange were happening to you."- 1 Peter 4:12

Read and reflect on Matthew 11:28-30

Are you feeling heavy laden? Who can give you rest?

Do you know what a yoke is used for? Look it up online or in a dictionary. It seems contradictory to take up a yoke to find rest. Reflect on this here.

What are you to do to find rest for your soul?

What do you need to learn from Jesus?

Read and reflect on Psalm 25.

Take some time to copy here or into your own journal a few verses that really minister to you.

What do you need from God today?

Future

The future will mean different things to each of you reading this.

For me, the future meant a lifetime without my son and a new sense of "normal." Less than a year later, God blessed us with another son, Nicholas, who had been born in Russia just months after Tommy. Truly, Nick has been used by the Lord in a powerful way to heal many of my wounds.

Initially, I was pessimistic and bitter. I felt like Job, persecuted from all sides. But, with time, I have come to see my life as part of a greater plan. I find that I trust God more deeply than I ever could have before. I know that He is in control and for that I am thankful. Though this is a daily battle I still fight, I am able to fight it with the wisdom I've gained through this trial.

Nine years after Tommy was born, my older sister, Kristan, gave birth to her fifth son, Jesse. Not realizing that anything was wrong, they were preparing to take him home from the hospital. Suddenly their nurse grew alarmed when she noticed Jesse's lips were blue. After being air-lifted to Denver Children's Hospital and spending a week in the hospital, tests confirmed that Kristan's youngest son had Down Syndrome.

At three months of age, Jesse spent three days on life support when he went into cardiac arrest following heart surgery. He then spent another month in the hospital while we pleaded and prayed for his healing. Praise God that Jesse has made a full recovery. Yes, he is developing at a slower rate, as would be expected, but he is nonetheless growing in wisdom and stature every day.

Kristan's story is different than mine, just as your story is different than mine. Kristan didn't know ahead of time that her son would have ongoing medical needs. She enjoyed a relatively carefree nine months of pregnancy, while I faced the confusion and grief of carrying a baby who might not survive.

My dear sister now faces the daily struggles of caring for a child with physical and mental special needs. Yet, she also has the daily joys of watching him light up with excitement when they go play baseball together and hearing him ask for "*i-meme*" (ice cream) in the sweetest little voice.

Truly, Jesse is a great blessing to us all and we are incredibly thankful to the Lord for him.

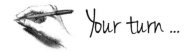 Your turn ...

How has your view of God, your life and the world changed since you were first aware something was wrong with your unborn child?

How has God brought healing to your heart?

When you envision the future, what do you see?

Read and reflect on Jeremiah 29:10-14.

So many people have heard Jeremiah 29:11 before, "For I know the plans I have for you, declares the Lord, plans for welfare and not for evil, to give you a future and a hope." It is a "coffee cup verse" which people like to throw around to encourage others ... and truly, what a blessing it is that the Lord has plans for our good! Please, though, take a moment to look at the context here with me.

What happened to the Israelites for <u>70 years</u> before the Lord's promise to them was fulfilled? (See Jeremiah 29:1 & 4)

Reread verse 14, what are God's plans for the Israelites' future?

What does this mean to you?

Did the Israelites enjoy year after year of unending joy and freedom from pain? No. They didn't.

In our human lives, it often takes trials and pain to bring about a hope and a future. How have you seen that in your own life?

Read and reflect on John 14:1-4

Where is Jesus now?

What is He doing there?

Read and reflect on Philippians 1:12-26

Paul is such an inspiration. Where is Paul when he is writing this letter to the Philippians? (v. 14)

In Philippians 1:20, what does Paul hope for?

Copy Philippians 1:21 here.

Paul goes on to say that he has a hard time choosing between wanting to die and wanting to live. Have you ever felt that way? Describe.

Why is it more necessary for Paul to remain in the flesh? (v. 22, 24)

How about you? Why is it necessary for you to remain in the flesh?

Let's return once again to Philippians 4:4-13. Reread and reflect on this passage.

Reread Philippians 4:6 and fill in the missing words:

"Do not be _____ about anything; but

in _____ by _____ and

_____ with _____ let

your requests be made known to _____."

Which of these directions are hardest for you? Explain.

In Philippians 4:11-13, Paul shares that he has learned to be content in any situation.

What is his secret?

Who strengthens Paul?

Do you feel that strength in your own life?

Write out the struggles you're having now and lift them up to the Lord.

Read and reflect on Psalm 116.

Take some time to copy here or into your own journal a few verses that really minister to you.

Write your own sacrifice of praise and thanksgiving to the Lord here.

In Closing

Dear Friend,

I pray that this study has blessed you as it has blessed me.

I am thankful that God created YOU. I am thankful that God created your child. I am thankful that God created Tommy. And I am now able to be thankful that He chose to take Tommy home.

Since Tommy's death, our family has been blessed with three more children. Our son, Nick, was adopted from Russia the following year. Five years later, I gave birth to another daughter (Noelle) and three more years later, another son (Daniel). I am not the same woman I was before walking this journey. The Lord has indeed blessed me, blessed us, beyond all we could even ask or imagine.

I'd love to hear from you. Please send me an email and visit my blog at www.TeachWhatIsGood.com

Truly,

Kim
kim@teachwhatisgood.com

My Prayer for Each of You

I pray that your future will hold beauty for ashes, gladness for mourning, and praise for despair. (Isaiah 61:3)

I pray that you might be granted that peace of God that surpasses all understanding and that His peace will guard your hearts and your minds in Christ Jesus, being anxious about nothing, but rather by prayer and supplication with thanksgiving you would let your requests be made known to God. (Philippians 4:6-7)

I pray that, though your future might not be the same "happily ever after" dream you might have dreamed as a little child, that the Lord would bless you with new and greater dreams, as you trust that His ways and His thoughts are higher than your own. (Isaiah 55:9)

I pray that you would trust in the Lord with all your heart and lean not on your own understanding. (Proverbs 3:5)

I pray that you would rejoice always, and pray without ceasing and give thanks in everything, knowing that this is indeed the will of God for you in Christ Jesus. (1 Thessalonians 5:16-18)

I pray that you would look to Jesus, the founder and perfecter of our faith, who for the joy set before Him endured the cross, despising the shame, so that you may not grow weary or faint hearted. (Hebrews 12:2-3)

From my Family to Yours,

"Grace to you and peace from God our Father and the Lord Jesus Christ.

Blessed be the God and Father of our Lord Jesus Christ, the Father of mercies and God of all comfort, who comforts us in all our affliction, so that we may be able to comfort those who are in any affliction, with the comfort with which we ourselves are comforted by God. For as we share abundantly in Christ's sufferings, so through Christ we share abundantly in comfort too. If we are afflicted, it is for your comfort and salvation; and if we are comforted, it is for your comfort, which you experience when you patiently endure the same sufferings that we suffer. Our hope for you is unshaken, for we know that as you share in our sufferings, you will also share in our comfort.

For we do not want you to be unaware, brothers, of the affliction we experienced in Asia. For we were so utterly burdened beyond our strength that we despaired of life itself. Indeed, we felt that we had received the sentence of death. *But that was to make us rely not on ourselves but on God who raises the dead.* He delivered us from such a deadly peril, and he will deliver us. On him we have set our hope that he will deliver us again." -- 2 Corinthians 1:2-10

About the Author

A college valedictorian and self-proclaimed "brainiac" with a Bachelor's degree in Education of the Hearing Impaired, Kim came to faith in Jesus Christ at 21 years of age. Life moved quickly from that point, caring for her computer guy husband, Bill, and ever growing family. A native of Des Moines, Iowa, she has made the greater Memphis area her home since 2006.

Following the stillbirth of her son, Tommy, in 1998, she founded "A Child of Promise," an online ministry supporting families continuing their pregnancies following an adverse prenatal diagnosis. You can find ACOP on the web at www.AChildOfPromise.org

A CLASS-Services trained speaker, Kim delights in opening her heart to ladies as she shares from God's Word how God transformed her life from an "evangelical atheist" into a sold out servant of Jesus Christ. Sharing from her unique experiences of brokenness, she engages listeners as they learn to live the life that God has for them through following Christ no matter the cost.

Read her blog at www.TeachWhatIsGood.com

> *"[Older women] are to teach what is good, and so train the young women to love their husbands and children, to be self-controlled, pure, working at home, kind, and submissive to their own husbands, that the word of God may not be reviled."* -- Titus 2:4-5

45042807R00060

Made in the USA
Lexington, KY
16 September 2015